FUTURE READY
RESEARCH PAPERS

LYRIC GREEN AND ANN GRAHAM GAINES

Enslow Publishing
101 W. 23rd Street
Suite 240
New York, NY 10011
USA
enslow.com

This edition published in 2018 by Enslow Publishing, LLC
101 W. 23rd Street, Suite 240, New York, NY 10010

Library of Congress Cataloging-in-Publication Data

Names: Green, Lyric, author. | Gaines, Ann, author.
Title: Future ready research papers / Lyric Green and Ann Graham Gaines.
Description: New York : Enslow Publishing, 2018. | Series: Future ready project skills | Includes bibliographical references and index. |
Audience: Grade 4 to 6.
Identifiers: LCCN 2017001299| ISBN 9780766086616 (library-bound) | ISBN 9780766087736 (pbk.) | ISBN 9780766087743 (6-pack)
Subjects: LCSH: Report writing--Juvenile literature. | Research—Juvenile literature.
Classification: LCC LB1047.3 .G745 2018 | DDC 371.30281--dc23
LC record available at https://lccn.loc.gov/2017001299

Printed in China

To Our Readers: We have done our best to make sure all website addresses in this book were active and appropriate when we went to press. However, the author and the publisher have no control over and assume no liability for the material available on those websites or on any websites they may link to. Any comments or suggestions can be sent by email to customerservice@ enslow.com.

Portions of this book originally appeared in the book *Ace It! Ace Your Research Paper* by Ann Graham Gaines.

Photo Credits: Cover, pp. 4, 7, 11, 16, 29, 33, 38 dotshock/Shutterstock.com; p. 3 David Arts/Shutterstock.com; p. 5 Jon Feingersh/Blend Images/Getty Images; pp. 6, 10, 13, 22, 23, 26, 30, 35, 36, 41 vvlinkov/Shutterstock.com (adapted); p. 8 Marla Sweeney/The Image Bank/Getty Images; p. 9 Weekend Images Inc./E+/Getty Images; p. 12 Universal Images Group/Getty Images; p. 14 Camelot/A.collection/amana images/Getty Images; p. 17 mikkelwilliam/E+/Getty Images; p. 19 Andy Ryan/Taxi/Getty Images; p. 20 Caroline Seidel/DPA/Getty Images; p. 24 Education Images/Universal Images Group/Getty Images; p. 28 Brian Summers/First Light/Getty Images; p. 31 Drazen/E+/Getty Images; p. 34 Frederic Cirou/PhotoAlto Agency RF Collections/ Getty Images; p. 37 Dougall_Photography/E+/Getty Images; p. 39 Mark Edward Atkinson/Blend Images/Getty Images; p. 42 Fuse/Corbis/Getty Images.

CONTENTS

CHAPTER 1

SO YOU HAVE TO WRITE A RESEARCH PAPER

Your teacher has assigned you a research paper. It might seem like a lot of work. Where do you start? The first thing to know is the meaning of the word "research." To do research is to hunt for information about a topic. A topic is one general idea. For example, your topic could be whale sharks, Ariana Grande, or Old Faithful. When you collect information, organize it, and write about it, you are writing a research paper. Usually research papers are written for school. But you could also do research for a scout project, an online magazine, or just for fun. You might even turn your research paper into a different kind of presentation, like a poster or an oral report. Why do teachers ask students to write research papers? They know it will help you succeed in life. Doing research teaches you how to find and present information.

WHAT IS A RESEARCH PAPER, ANYWAY?

Writing research papers helps students become "independent learners." Independent learners can find information by themselves and learn about the things that interest them. Research helps students become good at problem solving.

Don't worry too much about your research paper. This book will give you clear, step-by-step instructions to get the job done. The first four steps of the research paper process are called prewriting. The prefix "pre-" means "before," so prewriting means "before writing." This is what you do when you are planning your final product. Imagine that you are mak-

Research papers are a way to learn new information about a topic. You will write many research papers in your life.

6 EASY STEPS FOR ACING YOUR RESEARCH PAPER

STEP 1: Understand Your Assignment
STEP 2: Choose Your Topic
STEP 3: Research
STEP 4: Make an Outline
STEP 5: Draft and Revise Your Paper
STEP 6: Peer Review and Publication

ing a salad. Before you create the salad, you need to figure out what ingredients you want to use, gather them, and chop them up. Prewriting is gathering and preparing the ingredients of your research paper.

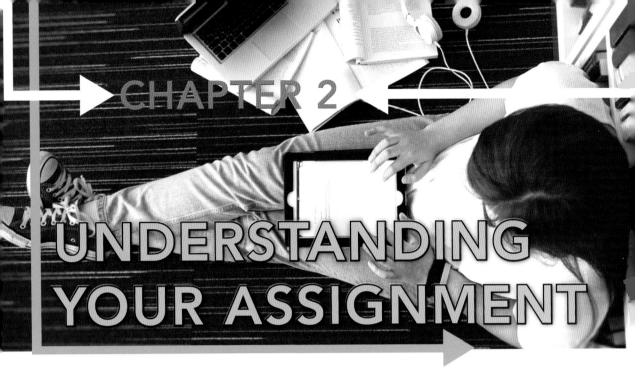

CHAPTER 2

UNDERSTANDING YOUR ASSIGNMENT

Before you begin writing, start with **Step 1**: Understand Your Assignment. Maybe your teacher wants you to write about the Amazon rain forest. Or, for your scout badge in astronomy, you have to write a big research paper about space. Maybe you've entered a local newspaper's essay contest.

KNOW WHAT YOU NEED TO DO

It's important to find out what kind of research you need to do. Your teacher might ask you to use a book, an encyclopedia, and a magazine article. Find out what your paper should look like. Should it have five paragraphs, or does it have to fill two pages? Do you have to type your paper on a computer? Do you need to include a title page, a bibliography, or illustrations?

Understanding your assignment will help you understand what kind of project you will be creating. It will also help you understand your topic better.

Some teachers will give you a useful tool called a rubric. This is a chart that your teacher will use to grade your paper. The chart lists all the requirements for your paper—things like a clear topic, excellent research, good organization, colorful illustrations, and so on. Your rubric is your guide to creating exactly what your teacher has assigned you. If you get a rubric, use it to understand your assignment. Keep it by your side every step of the way.

Do not leave Step 1 until you know your due date! Write it down on your calendar. Ask someone to remind you when the date gets close. Then make a timeline for your work. This will help you keep track of what needs to happen when. First, figure out how many days or weeks you have to finish your assignment. Cross out days when you won't be able to work

Make a schedule for your research paper. Sticking to your schedule will help you finish on time.

on your project. For a big project like a research paper, you need to break your work down into a series of small steps.

Here is how you should divide up the time you have for doing your paper:

10% brainstorming

25% researching and taking notes

20% making your outline

25% drafting your paper

20% revising, editing, and finishing your paper

RESEARCH PAPER TIMELINE

As soon as you get your assignment, make a timeline that says what you're going to do when. Copy this timeline in your research notebook. It will help you stay organized and on time.

Date my paper was assigned:_____

Due date:_____

Number of days (or weeks) I have to complete my paper:_____

Date I will begin work by brainstorming:_____

Date I will begin to do research and take notes:_____

Date I will begin to organize my notes and make an outline:_____

Date I will begin to write a draft of my paper:_____

Date I will begin to revise and edit my paper:_____

Date I will start peer review:_____

Date I will turn in my paper:_____

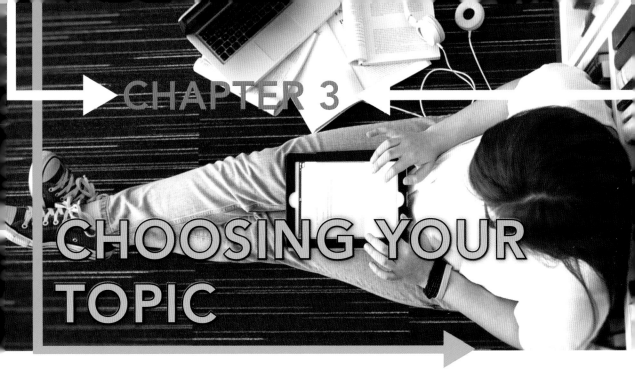

CHAPTER 3

CHOOSING YOUR TOPIC

Now that you understand your assignment, you are ready for **Step 2**: Choosing Your Topic. If you're assigned to write about animals, you know your general topic. Now you have to get more specific. You need to choose what kind of animal you want to write about. If you don't get specific, you'll end up with a very large topic. You'll gather too much information. Your paper will be too long and too hard to organize. You might want to focus on tiny animals. That topic is still too big. Think smaller. Try to think of just one tiny animal you want to learn about.

Now it is time for brainstorming. Make a list of all the ideas that come into your head. Still stuck? Do a little reading. You could browse in an encyclopedia or a big book about animals. Maybe you'll become interested in animals that live in groups. Now, narrow your topic even more. Finally, you might

Pygmy marmosets would make an interesting topic.

decide to write about the pygmy marmoset. These animals live in family groups in the treetops of the Amazon rain forest.

Next, ask yourself questions about the topic you have chosen. Ask yourself what you want to know more about. Maybe you wonder why the pygmy marmoset lives in groups. You might want to know more about how these animals communicate with each other.

But be careful! Make sure your topic isn't too small. A topic that's too specific is as bad as a topic that's too general. For example, let's say you choose the topic of where armadillos live. You won't find enough information to make a good paper. Your paper will be too short!

THE WRONG KIND OF TOPIC

Look for a topic that's not too big or too small. Make sure it's interesting and matches your assignment, too! Here are some topics that won't make a good research paper.

1. *Animals in the Amazon rain forest:* There are far too many animals that live in the Amazon. Your paper would take forever

WATCH OUT FOR PROCRASTINATION!

Do you procrastinate? That means putting work off until the last minute. If you wait too long to start work on a project, you can't do a good job. Experts give these tips to procrastinators:

- Block off time to work on your project. On your calendar, look for time when you will be free to work. Decide how many hours you'll work on those days.
- Sit by yourself when you work on a writing project. It will be hard to work if you have friends or family around. Try to find a quiet place where you can work alone.
- Avoid distractions. Turn off the television and any music while you work. If you have a cell phone, do not answer it unless it is your parents or an actual emergency.
- Expect the unexpected! Put aside extra time, just in case your family's plans change. Let's say your mom can't take you to the library on Thursday night. Saturday afternoon could be your backup plan.
- If you start worrying that you'll never finish, break down your project into small steps. This will make it easier and will help you feel calmer.

Think about your topic before you start your research. You don't want something too broad or too narrow!

to write! It would also probably be too long and very difficult to organize into clear thoughts.

2. *What blue whales eat:* Since blue whales only eat plankton, this topic is way too small.

3. *Bears in winter:* These animals hibernate during the winter, so this paper would be pretty boring!

CHAPTER 4

RESEARCH

N ow that you've picked your topic, it's time for **Step 3:** Research. While you do your research, you should think of yourself as a detective collecting evidence. First, think about where to find sources. Sources provide information. When your parents or grandparents did research, sources were printed—they were books, magazines, or newspapers.

Today, we have electronic sources, too, like websites and databases. There are even more types of sources. For example, if you need information about the civil rights movement, your own grandmother could be a source of information. You could ask her what it was like to live during that time in history. Sometimes, you can find sources for your research at home. You could look up information on your computer or in your own books. The best place to do research, though, is your school or public library.

Doing research is like investigating a mystery. Finding the answers to your questions makes you like a detective!

THE LIBRARY

At the library, start by using the catalog. All libraries have their catalogs on computers. Before you use the catalog, think of some keywords related to your topic. They will help you find useful sources. For a paper about pygmy marmosets, you might use keywords such as "pygmy marmoset," "rain forest," or "mammals."

Type your keywords into the library catalog's search box. Press ENTER. The computer will show you a list of sources about your keywords. For a book, you will see its title and call number. This number tells a librarian where to put the book on the library shelf. You can use it to find the book. To find magazine articles, ask a librarian to help you use the Readers' Guide to Periodical Literature or special magazine databases. As you explore the library, remember that librarians are expert detectives. They will help you learn how to use the library. They will also guide you to the materials you need.

As you conduct your research, keep thinking like a detective. Look for clues that lead you to useful information. The first books you find might not have what you want. Good researchers think like detectives.

They might be too simple or too hard to read. One way to find just the right sources is to browse. That means to look through the shelves until something catches your eye. When you find a book by its call number, look at other books nearby. They might help you, too! Browse inside sources, too. You do not need to read every word at first. Flip through a book or magazine article to see if it has helpful information or interesting illustrations. Remember, a picture or map can provide just as much information as words can.

INTERNET RESEARCH

The internet can also be a useful source. To get started, look at your list of keywords. At a computer with internet access, type in the name of a search engine. This is a website that provides sources of information. Google.com and AskKids.com are good search engines. Type your keywords into the search

The library is a great place to start researching the topic of your research paper.

box, and press ENTER. You will see a results page—a list of websites that include your keywords. Click on a link— a word or phrase that is usually in another color that leads to another site. Scan the website for useful information. If you find some information that is useful, you can print it out or take notes in a notebook.

You can also use personal experiences as research. Have you ever seen your topic in person, like at the zoo?

Once you're done with that one, go back to your results page and look at other sites. Both websites and printed sources often provide clues that lead you to other sources. In printed sources, flip to the end and look for a Further Reading list or bibliography. Many websites contain links to other helpful sites.

THE RIGHT KINDS OF RESEARCH

Taking notes is an important part of the research process. Look for information that answers the questions you have about your topic. If you are lucky, you will find many good sources. Soon you will have to choose exactly which ones to use. To do so, you'll need to evaluate the sources. That means you'll decide whether they really are good sources to use for your research project. A good source is relevant. That means it is closely related to your topic. If you're writing about armadillos in Texas, an article about armadillos in South America isn't relevant to your topic. One good way to find out if a book is relevant is to look at its table of contents. The table of contents is at the front of a book. It tells you the number of chapters.

Look at the table of contents for important clues about how a book is organized. You can also go to the very back of a book to find the index. That's an alphabetical list of the topics inside a book. The index tells you what pages to turn to for information about each topic. To use an index, look for your keywords in the alphabetical list. As you evaluate a source,

TIPS FOR STAYING SAFE ONLINE

The internet is a great place to find information. After all, surfing the Web is tons of fun. Unfortunately, it can also be dangerous. If you find a website that makes you uncomfortable, leave! When you're online, you might be asked to register for a website or to become a member of a group. Ask a trusted adult before you follow the instructions. You must never give out personal information unless a parent or teacher says it's okay. Personal information includes things like your name, address, phone number, email address, and the name of your school. Never send a photograph of yourself to a website. Do not respond to mean messages. If someone you talk to online wants to meet you in person, do not reply. Show the message to a trusted adult. He or she will let you know if it's okay to write back.

decide whether its information is factual—based on the **truth. You should** not use a work of fiction to write a research paper. Also, beware—the author of your source may sometimes state opinions rather than facts. You can include both facts and opinions in your research paper, but make sure you know which is which. For example, no one could really argue with the fact that strawberry is a flavor of ice cream. But someone might disagree with your opinion that strawberry is the best flavor of ice cream!

Finally, check to make sure your source is up to date. Old sources can lose their accuracy fast! It's really important to evaluate websites. Keep in mind that they are not always reliable. After all, absolutely anyone can post information on the internet. Usually, the best websites are created by experts. To find out who created a website, try looking at the bottom of the home page or click on a link called Contact Us. In one of those places, you often see the name of a person (like scientist Neil Degrasse Tyson) or an organization (like Stanford University). If you see a university, school, or museum, that's an excellent sign that you have found a good website.

Website addresses end with two or three letters that come after a period, or dot. This ending is called a domain extension. Extensions tell you what type of website you are visiting. Here's a guide to some common domain extensions. Notice that two-letter extensions stand for countries outside of the United States.

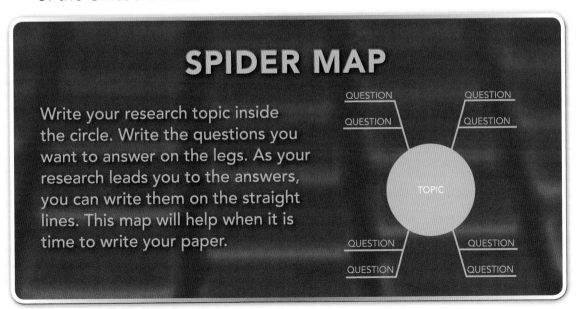

SPIDER MAP

Write your research topic inside the circle. Write the questions you want to answer on the legs. As your research leads you to the answers, you can write them on the straight lines. This map will help when it is time to write your paper.

QUESTION QUESTION
QUESTION QUESTION
TOPIC
QUESTION QUESTION
QUESTION QUESTION

The internet is a great place to research your topic.

.com commercial: used by businesses and companies

.edu education: used by schools such as public schools, colleges, and universities

.gov government: used by town, city, state, and national governments

.org organization: used by churches and charitable institutions

.ca Canada

.ru Russia

.uk United Kingdom

TAKING NOTES

Once you have decided which sources to use, you need to take notes. Good notes help you remember the information you find. They also help you organize your information and tell you where you found it. Notes are very important later, too, when it is time to create a bibliography for your paper. People have different ways of taking notes. Some write by hand on lined note cards. Some use a notebook.

Others like to take notes by typing them on a computer. Your teacher might tell you which way to take notes. Otherwise, choose the method you like most. People also differ in when they take notes. You can take notes as you read. Another way is to read through a chapter or article and then go back to take notes. Again, experiment with several ways and choose what works best for you. When you take notes, you usually should not copy down complete sentences. Write only a few words to remind you about a fact or idea. Rephrase the author's words. That means to write them in a different way, using your own words.

Sometimes, you will find a sentence that you really like. Maybe you want to quote these exact words in your paper. To quote means to copy someone else's words. When you quote an author in a research paper, you must tell your reader who wrote or spoke the words. In your notes, mark these words with quotation marks (" "). If you copy someone's words without telling your readers what you're doing, you plagiarize. If you plagiarize, you are cheating.

It is a good idea to label your notes with a topic. For example, on one note card—or in one section of a computer document—you could record facts about pygmy marmoset babies. On a different note card or document, write facts about what pygmy marmosets eat. Mark your notes with subject headings such as "Babies" or "What pygmy marmosets eat."

Along with your notes for each fact or quote, identify the source where you found it. Since you'll also be keeping a separate list of all your sources (more on this later), you could just use an abbreviation such as the author's last name or a short version of the title. Be sure to also write down the page number. Research papers end with a bibliography, or a list of sources used. This list of source notes gives specific information about each source you used, such as the author name, book title, and page number. There are different ways to write a bibliography. Your teacher or librarian can help you decide on the right way if your assignment did not include specific instructions. Use the graphic organizer on the next page to help record information for your bibliography.

AVOIDING PLAGIARISM

Plagiarism happens when you do not write your paper all by yourself. Instead, you use other people's words without saying so. That can happen if you're not very careful when you take notes. Never copy exact sentences from a source unless you see something that you really want to quote. If you do quote someone else's words, use quotation marks (" ") around the words. Write the name of the person who said them. Include the source in your bibliography. Teachers see plagiarism as a very serious problem. If they believe students have plagiarized, they often give students a failing grade. When you reach high school and college, plagiarism can get you kicked out of school. If you want help making sure you haven't plagiarized by accident, ask your teacher or a librarian.

SOURCE NOTES FOR MY BIBLIOGRAPHY

Copy this organizer onto another piece of paper to help you record source notes for your bibliography.

FOR A BOOK

Author(s) (last name, then first name):

Title:

Copyright date (find this on the copyright page):

Name of publisher (from the copyright page):

FOR A MAGAZINE ARTICLE

Author(s) (last name, then first name):

Article title:

Magazine title:

Date article was published:

Page numbers:

FOR AN INTERNET ARTICLE

Author or organization's name (if you can't find it):

Name of the Web page:

URL (the Web page address):

Date you first looked at the article:

FOR AN ENCYCLOPEDIA ARTICLE

Name of the article (entry name):

Title of the encyclopedia:

Copyright date:

After you take notes, sort them. Put them into an order that makes sense. For example, you might want to group information about pygmy marmoset's fingers with tree climbing, since they use their fingers to soar through the trees. As you look at your notes and sort them, you might come up

To write the best research paper, you should use all the resources at your disposal. Go to the library to look for book sources, and use the internet to use web sources. Your research will be well-rounded and you'll find more information on your topic!

with new questions about your topic. If that happens, do a bit more research and find the answers.

Now is also a good time to reach some conclusions about your topic. You draw conclusions when you put together clues to figure out something new. For example, if you find that each group of pygmy marmosets stays in a small area, you might conclude pygmy marmosets live in areas with lots of trees. Your con-clusion is what you want your reader to remember about your research paper.

Each of your note cards should have a clear subject. Try not to put too much informa-tion on one card. Always use your own words when taking notes, unless you want to use a whole quote. When you do use a quote, be sure and name your source.

CHAPTER 5

ORGANIZING AN OUTLINE

You'll have a much easier time writing if you organize your paper first. Decide on a main idea for each paragraph. You will identify each main idea in a topic sentence. Then you'll add details to fill out each paragraph.

GET IT IN ORDER

There's more than one way to get your ideas in order. One way is to move on to **Step 4:** Make an Outline. Whichever method you use, it will help you get organized and give you a plan. An outline is an organizer. You use numbers and letters to put information in ordered groups. You can see an example of an outline on page 32.

When you use a mind map, you organize your information in a visual way. Write your topic in a circle in the center of a piece of paper. Surround that circle with other circles, and write your main ideas. Add details on branches connected to your main idea circles.

MIND MAP

MAIN IDEAS What they look like
Live in trees
Pygmy marmosets communicate with each other through contact calls
Gumnivores - eat tree gum

TOPIC Pygmy marmosets

DETAILS Special teeth for getting gum out of trees
Live in families of up to nine, males carry babies on their backs
Live in the Amazonian rain forest
Threatened by loss of habitat
Some kept as exotic pets
Mate for life
Females hunt for food
Males take care of children and look out for predators

As you work on your outline or mind map, you might discover that some of your information doesn't belong. That's okay. Don't use it. On the other hand, you might discover that you have some new questions. Then you need to do more research. Take time to fill in your gaps. In your outline or mind map, you can include more than just main ideas and details. For example, show where you want to add quotations, maps, charts, or photographs. You can use an outline like the one on the next page to plan your research paper.

THE BEGINNING AND THE END

Research papers start with an introduction. It says what your paper is about. Think about how to get your reader interested. You could begin with a question or a fun fact. Research papers end with a conclusion. That's where you sum up what you know. Think about what you want your reader to remember.

Keep your notes organized while you research. It will make writing your paper easier later.

Make sure it is exciting! Introductions and conclusions can be hard to write. You might want to write them after you've written the rest of your paper.

A GOOD PYGMY MARMOSET OUTLINE

I. Introduction
II. What do they look like?
    A. Size
        1. Body only 4-6 in (102 to 152 mm) long, tail twice as long
        2. Fur is brown, gold, and gray
    B. Gumnivore
        1. Special teeth for eating gum from trees
III. Range and habitat
    A. Rain forests of the Amazon Basin (include map here)
    B. Each family has its own territory
        1. Live in the treetops
    C. Mothers hunt for food while fathers watch the babies and look out for predators
    D. Live in family groups of up to nine
        1. Pygmy marmosets can talk! (sort of)
    E. Communicate through calls and sounds
VI. Conclusion: pygmy marmosets are more like us than we think!

Outlines aren't written in complete sentences. The writer lists specific and necessary details only.

CHAPTER 6

WRITE AND REVISE

Now that you're researched and organized your thoughts, you're ready for **Step 5**: Draft and Revise Your Paper. A draft is a first version—a try. It can be tricky to get started. If words don't come to you right away, reread your notes. As you write, follow your outline or mind map. Remember to give every paragraph a topic sentence telling its main idea. Then add details. When you draft, don't worry about making every sentence perfect. You will do that soon enough. As you draft, mark words you're not sure how to spell or facts you want to check. You can use a pen, a sticky note, a highlighter, or a bracketed note [like this one].

Once you've done your research, you can begin drafting your paper.

REVISING

Once you're done with your draft, you're ready to revise and edit your paper. This is your chance to improve your paper. But you don't have to change everything. Revision is like polishing the rough parts of the paper. Before you begin to revise, it's a good idea to review your instructions. If your teacher gave you a rubric, look at it. Make sure that your paper matches the assignment. Next, look at your draft. Read it aloud. This will help you find out if your words make sense. Mark changes you want to make with a colored pencil or highlighter, or use the highlight feature in your word processing program. You might decide to rewrite sentences or move some around. This is your chance to make your paper exciting. Cut parts that do not connect to your main ideas. Take out boring facts. Also,

PARAGRAPH SKETCH

Write your main idea in a large box. Write details that support the main idea in smaller boxes. If a detail does not support the main idea, leave it out! When you are done marking changes you want to make, either neatly rewrite your paper by hand or go back onto the computer to fix it. Don't forget to save your new work if you are using a computer!

WRITER'S BLOCK

"Writer's block" describes the frustrating feeling of being unable to write. You might get writer's block if you don't understand what to do, if you haven't done enough research, or if you find your paper boring. To get over writer's block, review the assignment. Dig up more exciting details. Then focus on one paragraph—or even just one sentence—at a time. Try asking your teacher or another adult to look at your draft. Then you can see if you're on the right track. It can also help just to talk about your topic with a friend or family member. This can help make you feel more confident about how much you have learned and how much you have to say.

Proofreading is a very important part of the writing process! Check for more than punctuation and spelling. Make sure you're using the right form of each word, too!

think about your word choice. Make sure you aren't using the same word over and over again.

Next, proofread your paper. That means checking your capitalization, spelling, and punctuation. If you aren't sure where your errors are, check a dictionary, thesaurus, or grammar book. You can also ask your teacher for help. Now is another good time to review your assignment and rubric. Make sure you've done everything the rubric says.

CHAPTER 7

PEER REVIEW AND PUBLISHING

Y ou've chosen your topic. You've done your research. You've created your outline. You've drafted and revised your paper. Now it's time for **Step 6:** Peer Review and Publication.

PEER REVIEW

Do you want your research paper to be really good? Find a partner and try a peer review.

In a peer review, you ask a friend or classmate to read your paper. Ask your partner to tell you how you could make your paper better. Try not to get upset if she points out a place where you made a mistake. After all, that's what peer review is for. It is better to find out now than to get a lower grade on your paper!

When it's your turn to give a peer review, think before you speak. Point out parts you don't understand. Be careful to talk about the writing and not the person who wrote it. Be specific. Don't say, "You did a bad job here." Instead, say something like, "This section is confusing. I don't understand what an incisor is." Don't go overboard when you criticize. Also, it's very important to remember to praise the writer! Talk about the parts you find easy to read or exciting.

Your friends can help make your paper better, too. Listen to them when they offer suggestions. Be sure and offer to read their papers, too!

FINAL TOUCHES

After you've gotten your peer review, make some final changes. Then it's time to think about how your finished paper will look. Make sure it is neat and you have at least 1-inch margins around the edges of each piece of paper. Next, add your extras. First, create your title page. It should include your first and last name, the title of your paper, and the class you're in (or the contest you're entering). Your bibliography goes on its own page. Arrange your sources in an alphabetical list by the authors' last names. You can also add illustrations, maps, or charts to your paper. If you've drawn your own illustrations, sign your name. If you've copied them from somewhere else, write the name of the source below the illustration.

WHAT NOW?

Once you've finished your paper, you might want to do more than just turn it in. You could send it to your school newspaper or an online magazine. You might be able to turn it into a display for the wall in your classroom or the exhibit case at your library. Once you're all done, it's time for evaluation. If you've written your paper for school, your teacher will give it a grade. Talk with your teacher to find out what he or she liked about it—and what you could have done better. It's a great

EVALUATE YOURSELF

Self-evaluation can help you figure out what went right and wrong with your research paper. Copy these questions on another piece of paper, and write down your answers.

How did I find my best sources?
What did I do best on this project? (for example, research or illustrations)
What did I want to learn from this project?
What did I learn?
What will I do differently next time?

If you follow all the steps in this book, you're sure to ace your research paper!

Hannah A Edwards
History / Geography
Miss Coven
5 C

A+

idea to think about how you think the project went, too. You can use an evaluation form like the one on page 41 to reflect on your own work. Evaluate yourself honestly each time you do a research paper. Then your research and writing skills will improve every time. This will be a wonderful reason to celebrate!

GLOSSARY

bibliography A list of sources used in a piece of writing.

brainstorm To come up with ideas and write them down as they pop into your head.

browse To look through something quickly without reading every word.

call number A number that tells where a book should go on the library shelf.

catalog A collection of cards or a computer database that lists everything a library holds.

conclusion A statement that sums up or makes a judgment about something.

copyright page The page in a book that says who published it, where, and when. It is usually near the front of the book.

draft To write the first version of a paper.

evaluate To decide if something is good or bad.

evidence Facts that prove a statement or support a main idea.

fiction Writing that tells a made-up story.

home page A website's main page.

index An alphabetical list of topics inside a book.

keyword A word or phrase used to search for information.

margin A blank space along the edge of a piece of paper.

oral report A speech that gives an audience information about a certain topic.

plagiarize To take someone else's work without giving credit. Instead, you say it is your own.

prewriting Preparing and organizing before drafting a paper.

proofread To check writing for mistakes in grammar, punctuation, and spelling.

quote To use someone else's exact words.

relevant Directly related to a certain topic.

reliable Dependable and accurate.

rephrase To say something in a different way, in your own words.

research To search for information about a particular topic.

research paper A written paper where the topic is researched to present information.

rubric A chart that tells what a piece of writing should include.

search engine A website that helps you search for information on other websites.

sources Books, newspapers, websites, and other places to find information.

table of contents The list of chapter titles and page numbers in the front of a book or other publication.

topic Subject or main idea; what you are writing, reading, or speaking about.

topic sentence The sentence that tells the topic of a paragraph.

URL A website address, usually beginning with "http://" or "www."

FURTHER READING

BOOKS

Graham, Leland, and Isabelle McCoy. *How to Write a Great Research Paper*. Chicago, Ill: Incentive Publications by World Book, 2014.

Greenberg, Michael. *Painless Study Techniques*. Hauppauge, NY: Barron's Educational Publishing, 2016.

Jakubiak, David J. *A Smart Kid's Guide to Doing Internet Research*. New York, NY: PowerKids Press, 2009.

San Francisco Writers' Grotto. *642 Things to Write About—Young Writer's Edition*. San Francisco, Ca: Chronicle Books, 2014.

WEBSITES

American Library Association
http://gws.ala.org
A list of recommended sites for kids on many topics.

Jumpstart.com
http://www.jumpstart.com/parents/activities/essay-writing
-activities
Tips for writing an essay.

Time for Kids
http://www.timeforkids.com/homework-helper/a-plus-papers
/persuasive-essay
Tips for writing a persuasive essay.

INDEX